BONSAI

An Essential and Comprehensive Guide to Growing, Wiring, Pruning and Caring for Your Bonsai Tree

by
Akira Kobayashi - 小林明

TABLE OF CONTENTS

The term bonsai, from the Japanese *bon* (pot) and *sai* (tree), indicates an art form that allows you to grow miniature trees and plants, through meticulous daily care.

Originally, the bonsai spread to China where the skill of the masters reached the point of creating real tiny landscapes populated by mountains, rivers, houses, and people.

It is said that the poet Guen-Ming, in the fourth century after Christ, had retired to devote himself to planting and caring for chrysanthemums in some containers, thus starting the cultivation of plants in pots.

Two hundred years later, a new art was created in China, the Pen-Jin, as shown by various paintings of the Tang Dynasty (618-906), depicting dwarf trees used as ornaments.

During the 14th century, under the Ming Dynasty, bonsai were already widespread and were cultivated giving life to various styles.

However, bonsai is not only born as an aesthetic requirement but also as a spiritual exercise, as a search for harmony between man and nature, within the principles of the Zen discipline. The bonsai artist tests himself, brings his inner world closer to the outer one, trying to imprison and regulate the millennial forces of nature. In following his art, he is guided by the Zen concepts of naturalness, simplicity, harmony, and concentration on the essential.

When bonsai arrived in Japan, as a gift from wealthy Chinese, it fascinated the aristocracy precisely because of its spiritual intensity, thus becoming one of the nobility's favorite art forms. For Japan, this was the period of the spread of Zen Buddhism, during the Heian era, between the eighth and twelfth centuries.

Bonsai made their entrance into religious ceremonies and, over time, they were considered truly sacred symbols, to be venerated and cared for with assiduous and profound faith.

Only a few centuries later, bonsai ceased to be an elitist practice and was also freely spread among the people. Bonsai did not reach Europe until the end of the 19th century when commercial traffic with the east began to intensify. A Japanese exhibitor showed these unusual dwarf trees to the European public during the 1889 Paris World Cup, enjoying considerable success, interest, and curiosity among the numerous visitors.

Since then, bonsai has gathered passionate practitioners all over the world considered by some to be such an arduous art as to become magical, but in a really easy application for anyone with goodwill and patience.

The bonsai artist cultivates and takes care of his creation in a small container and trying to reproduce a glimpse of nature inside his home, which preserves the harmony of proportions, despite being significantly reduced in size.

He tries to draw its entire splendor from the plant, placing it in a landscape that resembles the real one for everything and enhancing its shape and qualities.

Like any plastic art, bonsai must also respect the basic principles of form, line, texture, space and color. The bonsai artist must always keep these concepts in mind to give value to his creation.

The form is any characteristic or structure that identifies a particular object. Even trees have their own shape, typical of the species they belong to; populate forests, woods and grasslands, adapting to the most diverse climates. Shapes and scenarios that we must strive to recreate in our bonsai.

The line establishes the border or boundary within which a work of art is created. For bonsai, limits are defined by the lines of the container, and the bonsai artist must learn to choose the suitable spatial boundaries within which to place his plant, highlighting its fundamental characteristics.

The texture is the set of structural qualities of a work of art and is born from how an artist works the chosen materials; even bonsai have their own texture, due to the structure of the leaves, the foliage, the trunk, etc.

In some compositions, therefore, some bonsai may be more appropriate than others for the characteristics of their texture: In case you want to highlight the knottiness of a trunk, for example, it is good to choose a tree with a particular bark, or if you want a contrast in the texture, you can combine deciduous trees with evergreen trees.

Space is defined, in art, as the extension that opens in all directions and in the three dimensions, within which things exist.

In bonsai, space is very important, both in the case of compositions, to establish the distance between the trees, and in the case of single trees, in order to obtain the right ratio inside container, space must, therefore, be dosed appropriately, avoiding disproportions or imbalances in the composition.

Finally, color is the sensation due to the stimulation of the retina by the light waves reflected by objects, which thus take on our eyes, particular characteristics and values.

Even bonsai have their colors, not only those of the trunk, leaves and flowers but also those dominant in the various seasons, such as the intermediate shades of the autumn and spring periods. All these elements must be taken into account during the realization of your project.

The bonsai artist must, however, also follow other rules, which allow you to set the creation and processing of any work of art. Let's talk about balance, rhythm, emphasis and unity.

The balance can be symmetrical or asymmetrical and implies certain stability of the figure. In bonsai art, however, symmetry is considered boring and therefore to be avoided. Rather, we try to give movement to the compositions and we tend to the variety of the form.

Rhythm implies a harmonious succession of the form so that the eye moves through the whole work, without interruption from start to finish.
The rhythm is very important for the bonsai that must hit the eye for its general appearance more than for some details, particularly interesting.

The emphasis gives particular relevance to a small part or to an entire area of an object. It can be obtained, either through the decision of the line, or through the specific use of color, or with lighting effects, or through the skillful use of details.

In bonsai, the emphasis can be used to highlight a feature of the plant that we particularly like, which will contribute to the movement of the composition.
Finally, the unit uses color, line, shape, texture and space to obtain a figure that satisfies us as a whole.

To achieve this, it is necessary that each of the elements mentioned completely harmonizes with the others.

By following these principles, a good bonsai artist can manage to obtain a bonsai of excellent value and remarkable value.

Before starting to describe the actual practical work, it is good to dwell a moment on some interesting distinctions that allow us to establish the first classification of bonsai.

It is important, in fact, to distinguish bonsai into two large groups:

Outdoor and indoor ones. The first are those who live in the open air without any particular damage.

They usually belong to species accustomed to climates characterized by significant changes in temperature and sudden changes of season.

The latter, however, are those that need a moderate and constant temperature to survive. To these belong many tropical and subtropical species, such as ficus, schefflera, jacaranda, which would live very little if left exposed to our climates. Therefore, it is always good to read up on the needs and climatic habits of the plant, so as to offer it the best possible living condition.

Bonsai trees are also classified according to their height, which can vary from a minimum of 6 inches to a maximum of 47 inches. The "miniature" bonsai do not exceed the height of 6 inches.

The "small" bonsai is less than 8.6 inches in size and are more readily available on the market. The "medium-small" bonsai reach the height of 16inches and for this, they are more easily cultivated. Then there are the "medium" bonsai that vary between 16 inches and 35 inches and the "large" ones, with a maximum height of 47 inches.

CHAPTER 1 - HOW TO GROW BONSAI

Those who are about to undertake the art of bonsai must keep in mind that it is a job that requires great attention and considerable patience, along with all the stages of development and growth of your bonsai, from the first moment of cutting the roots, the choice of the pot, the shape that the bonsai will have to take.

The beginner will not be able to immediately breed an excellent quality bonsai, but he will still be able to achieve many satisfactions managing to keep the size of the chosen tree or plant considerably reduced. The starting point of the work concerns the choice between the various ways to obtain a bonsai plant that meets our needs and abilities.

There are many ways to get a map that can serve our purposes; among the most common, we will remember: Bonsai taken in nature, grown from seed, multiplied by cutting, multiplied by layering, obtained by grafting, bonsai purchased in a nursery. In this order, the main rules to be observed for the best results will be listed.
In this order, the main rules to be observed for best results will be listed.

Recovered in nature or Yamadori

A rather easy way to get a plant is to take it directly in its natural environment: Going into a forest, it is often easy to find small plants that can meet our needs, requiring only the time of the pleasant walk.

Japan many bonsai, among the most famous for their beauty and seniority, like many black pines with five needles or junipers, were obtained with the Yamadori method.

However, not all the plants we encounter are suitable for becoming a bonsai, because, for various reasons, they would not grow in the right way, disappointing our expectations.

The first thing to do, therefore, is to consider only plants that show themselves as the most robust and healthy, with small leaves, uniformly arranged on the branches.

It is good to make sure that the roots are also strong and well developed, and that the branches have grown in many directions, to give an impression of movement. Overall, the plant should look strong, small but compact.

Once the plant is chosen, the most delicate phase is that of transplanting, so it is good to pay close attention to how the operation is performed. The recommended period is just before spring when the vegetation awakens and the climate softens.

The roots defend themselves better from damage and are more willing to take root easily in new soil. However, good results were also achieved in late spring, between April and May, especially in mountain areas, and in autumn. Here's how it goes. The soil around the tree is cleaned of blades of grass that hinder the work and those branches that will not serve our purpose or those that have grown excessively in length are cut, making the plant more manageable.

We then proceed to dig a circle corresponding to the circumference of the crown for a depth of about 6 inches, avoiding cutting the roots and possibly trying to take a plant whose root system is developed uniformly in every direction, which contributes to increasing the value of the bonsai.

If the plant is to be transported, the earth is sprayed with water and wrapped with damp gauze or newsprint, tying everything with twine in order to facilitate transport. It can be convenient to place the plant in a nylon bag that will also allow you to keep humidity constant. For a couple of months, waiting for the plant to resume all its functions, it is good to keep it in a normal pot with unfertilized soil, watering it abundantly and keeping it sheltered from wind and sun.

A perforated transparent plastic bell is recommended to limit evaporation. When it begins to throw the first shoots, then you can proceed with the repotting in a bonsai container.

Cultivation from seed or Misho

Bonsai from a plant taken in the wild

This is the decidedly more fascinating method as it allows the seedling to grow and to follow its development from its seed state; however, it is also the method that takes the longest time before truly embarking on the art of bonsai. Sometimes there is talk of several years.

The seeds can be found directly in nature, which implies a good one seed knowledge or purchased from a dealer. In both cases, it is important to bear in mind that some seeds need special care before they can be planted.

Some species must be subjected to a pre-germination period in which the seeds are left for 24 hours in a basin full of water, the fertile seeds will deposit on the bottom forfeiting water, and the others will remain on the surface.

Other species must spend a cool period, between 2 and 8 degrees Celsius - 46.4 Fahrenheit, to be able to mature. In any case, it would be good to seek advice from a gardener who can adequately inform us about the needs of the various species of seeds.

As for seeds to buy, the packs on which the word Bonsai is written are preferred, even if any seed can become a good bonsai. But now, let's continue the job description.

After making the first decisions on the choice of seed, proceed with sowing. The seedbed consisting of a small container filled with poor soil, which is without fertilizers (usually a mixture of sand and peat), is prepared. In this state, the seed is already in itself wrapped in sufficient nutrients to allow it to develop well.

The container should be filled up to 2 inches from the edge.

Once the moment of sowing has arrived (usually spring), proceed by burying the seeds with light pressure, the larger ones must be covered by at least 1inch of soil, the smaller ones by 0.5 inch.

If the size of the seed is really tiny then it will be sufficient to spread it regularly. We then begin to water them abundantly and gently, taking care not to create harmful grooves in the ground.

A solution with Chinosol can also be used. At this point, it would be useful to cover the container with a glass or plastic bell, so as to keep the soil at a certain humidity and temperature (the ideal one is 18-20 degrees Celsius - 64.4-68 Fahrenheit).

The container should be kept away from the sun, often watering the soil to prevent the seeds from drying out.

For this operation, the use of an inclined onion or a nebulizer is recommended, because, if the jet were too strong, it would move the earth and make the seeds float.

Once the seedlings are born, the bell can be removed and when the first leaves have sprouted, the transplant is carried out in a new container. It is important not to fertilize the land for at least a month.

After this period, the fertilizer will be administered in half the dose compared to that written on the pack.

When the height of the seedlings will be 4 inches, you can begin to act on the shape.

Multiplication by cuttings or Sashiki

This method consists of obtaining a new seedling using a part of an already formed plant. This allows us two main advantages: First, we can easily dispose of a lot of bonsai material, simply by removing the parts of the plant that interest us.

Secondly, the multiplication by cutting allows us to maintain the same characteristics typical of the mother plant with absolute fidelity also for the following generations.

However, even the cutting method while very easy to implement, is time-consuming. The cuttings are divided into four groups: It is possible to obtain a stem cutting, a sprouting cutting, a leaf-cutting and a root cutting.

The stem cutting, also called eda-zashi, uses already fully mature and robust branches. These, if buried or immersed in water, develop their own root system, becoming autonomous plants.

Therefore, branches not older than three years and which are not perishable due to disease or insects are to be chosen.

The branch must be around 8 inches long and must be cut immediately under a leaf node. The sprig must then be cleaned from the base by the leaves and planted in the ground, making sure that the shoots remain on the surface as much as needed. It must then be watered abundantly and covered with a glass or plastic plate.

It is important that during the first months the pot is in a bright place without being exposed to direct sun and that the soil is kept constantly humid. Once the first roots have sprouted, the seedling can be discovered from the slab and fertilized.

Transplanting into a bonsai container should only be done once the roots are fully formed to develop. The cutting from shoots, called shinme-zashi, uses a young shoot to develop a new plant.

The shoot must be cut obliquely with a sharp blade and must be leafless in the lowest part of its length. The other leaves, on the other hand, are simply to be checked by a third, so that evaporation is reduced to a minimum. Then the leafless stem of the bud is wrapped with a clay ball with a diameter of 1 inch, making sure that the lower part of the bud is positioned approximately in the center of the clay ball. You can finally proceed to bury the sprout up to completely cover the part wrapped in clay.

Leaf-cutting, or ha-zashi, consists of planting a sprig in the soil leaving a leaf on the surface. The soil must be watered carefully and kept away from the sun. The sprig will emit the roots and develop other leaves.

The root cutting, called ne-zashi, consists instead of gathering the roots of the chosen tree during the winter season and cutting them into 3 inches long pieces. A container should be prepared to contain damp sand, on which the roots will be placed and left to rest until spring. Important, to cover the container with a glass plate and leave it at a temperature of 2-4 degrees Celsius – 35,6-39,2 Fahrenheit.

When the roots begin to develop, transplanting can be carried out in suitable soil, making sure that the outermost part of the root is at ground level.

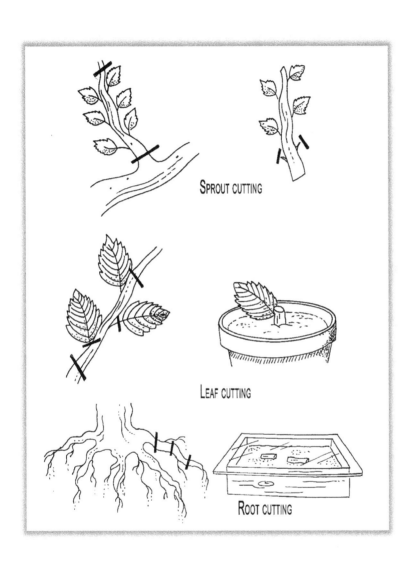

SPROUT CUTTING

LEAF CUTTING

ROOT CUTTING

Multiplication by layering or Toriki

Multiplication by layering consists of putting in contact a branch of the plant specially engraved with peat or earth, to make it root.

This is a method that allows you to obtain seedlings from rather large branches, in a short time, which would instead be very difficult to achieve by cutting.

The layering is recommended above all on some types of plants such as the Pomegranate, the Spruce, the Myrtle, the Maple, the Elm and the Cryptomeria, which have a great ability to develop roots both from the trunk and from the branches.

It is preferable to undertake the operation in the spring, even if good results are obtained at any time of the year. Let's see how it goes together.

Once the branch of the plant has been chosen, the lateral jets are removed for a short distance and engraved in the bark, forming a ring of about 1 inch in height around which the roots will form.

Two cuts from the bottom up to the sides of the branch can also be practiced, introducing a pebble or peat into the wound so that it does not close again.

There is also a third method of practicing the wound, consisting of wrapping two very close circles of wire tightly in the established point. In this way, with the growth of the tree, the wire will cut the bark gradually.

It is also important to sprinkle the wound with rooting hormone powder and prevent it from healing.

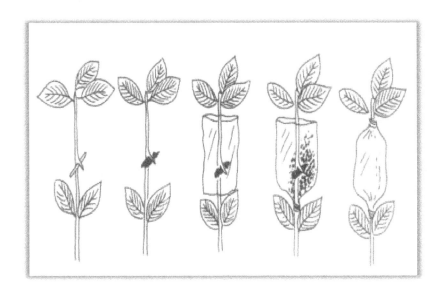

Layering Procedure

To obtain the roots, a transparent polyethylene sleeve stops under the incision, so as to create a funnel, and it is filled with peat to wrap the wound.

The sleeve is also closed over the incision with adhesive tape and the peat is constantly moistened. If the operation is unsuccessful, the branch will wither and die after a week or two; otherwise, the roots will begin to sprout.

When the root system is thick enough (usually 6-8 weeks), the new plant can be cut under the incision, placing it definitively in a container.
When the roots have well-rooted in the pot, you can proceed with the development of the bonsai.

Propagation by grafting or Tsugiki

Grafting is another way to get a bonsai plant. It consists of joining two different plants, to add their qualities into one. The plant on which the graft is practiced takes the name of "subject" or "portliness" (daiki), while the branch that is grafted is called "scion" or "grafting" (sugan: This process can be very useful for aesthetic purposes, to protect the plant from particular parasites, or to obtain a greater variety of fruit). In bonsai art, however, this method is often not recommended, especially the two types of grafting: A) *Basic grafting;* B) *Top grafting* to beginners, due to the special care and experience it requires.

The grafting is generally practiced during the spring and with very young trees, of two or three years, which manage to adapt more easily to the various situations.

Now let's see how the two main types of grafting are made: The top ones and the base ones. The top graft, also called ten-tsugi, is made in the upper part of a plant.

After having chosen the rootstock, it is truncated horizontally at the established point and a vertical cut is made which cuts the branch in half for about 1 inch.

The lower part of the scion must be prepared by removing the leaves and cutting it in the shape of a wedge, in this way it can perfectly adapt to the cut of the rootstock.

Now you need to join the two parts together, making sure that they fit together in the best way, so they must be tied well with a rope.

The basic graft, or moto-tsugi, concerns instead a lateral union that is practiced at the base of the trunk or branch of a plant.

In this case, we proceed in a slightly different way: The cut of the rootstock must be practiced literally from top to bottom for the depth of about 1 inch, creating a sort of notch in the trunk.

The cut of the scion must then be studied in an appropriate way to this notch, so as to fit perfectly into the rootstock, allowing quick healing of the wound.

Also, in this case, a strong binding will be necessary to facilitate the union of the two parts. Before transplanting it is good to cut the leaves in half and cut the main root.

This will assist in welding, limiting the growth of the rootstock.

Once practiced any of the two grafts it is good to place the plant in a place sheltered from the sun and drafts, watering to keep the soil moist, but without exceeding, so as not to rot the roots. After a month, the graft should begin to throw new shoots, then the binding must be eliminated and the soil fertilized in small doses.

However, the following factors should always be kept in mind.

Plants must be compatible: It is not possible to graft two plants that have too different characteristics, such as an apple tree and an orange.

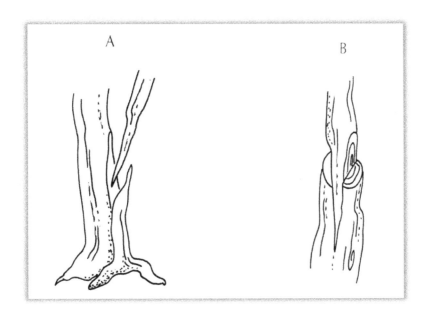

The part of the two plants that come into contact, called the change, must be carefully joined because nourishment passes from it to the upper plant. Never practice grafting in an unsuitable season, such as winter.

The direction of the buds of the scion must be the same as that of the rootstock, i.e., upwards.

A bonsai obtained by grafting, however, can begin to show good results only after a couple of years of careful care.

Buying the plant in a nursery is certainly the easiest way to start a bonsai, as it does not involve any of the risks mentioned above.

However, it excludes the great satisfaction of growing a bonsai from the early stages. It is very important, however, to carefully consider the plant you want to buy; it is easy, to come across rather expensive specimens that deserve careful consideration.

In order not to incur unpleasant accidents, we list the three main evaluation criteria of a bonsai, so that we can get an idea of the appropriate price:

The first characteristic is the age: The older a bonsai is, the higher its price will rise. However, it is well known that age is often increased during the purchase phase.

We recommend giving importance to age, but above all to focus on the aesthetic aspect of the plant we want to buy.

The general aspect of the bonsai is also important and must be healthy and vigorous.

During the purchase, therefore, it is necessary to consider the state of health and robustness of the tree, starting from the root system which must have well-developed rootlets, up to the branches and crown which must be proportionate and harmonious.

In this regard, it is good to know that if the bonsai has visible wounds; these do not diminish the value of the plant.

The important thing is that they are well healed and that they do not aesthetically ruin the general appearance.

The bonsai must have a simple shape, which respects the basic styles of which we will talk shortly.
It is therefore advisable to decide to buy the tree when you already have in mind the main characteristics that you want in bonsai, according to the style and species you have chosen.

Considering these criteria, we will be able to assess whether or not the price of a bonsai corresponds to its main characteristics.

Given the size and small thickness of many bonsai containers, there is often the risk that the plant will not be able to stand alone. It is therefore necessary to anchor it to have greater support.
There are two anchoring methods: The roots of the tree are stopped using metal wire at the bottom of the container.

This can be done in two ways: Either by tying the wire to the drainage metal mesh or by letting the wire come out of the drain hole and then stopping it under the pot.

In the case of group bonsai, only the largest trees will be anchored to the container, then tying to those smaller ones. Threads will be removed when the roots have developed sufficiently.

On the one hand, a moist mixture of potting soil and peat is prepared and wrapped, compressing it, around the roots of the tree, to weigh it down and make it more stable. It then ends by filling the container with normal soil.

CHAPTER 2- BONSAI AND ITS STYLES

Once the bonsai has found its definitive seat in the pot, you can devote yourself to the development of the aerial part of the plant.

To do this, bonsai requires continuous attention, ranging from pruning, topping, to the application of metal wire, etc.

All these operations contribute to giving the bonsai a particular shape.

In fact, in bonsai practice, there are many traditional styles that condition the shape of the crown, of the stem, and the branches of the tree according to specific rules.

Starting from the assumption that a bonsai is in all respects a miniature tree and that therefore has its own aesthetic harmony; the styles derive their reason of being from the careful observation and cataloging of the forms of their corresponding "giant cousins."

The bonsai artist tries in a few words to reproduce at bonsai level all those forms that over time nature has produced in normal trees.

Therefore, below we will cover the main styles that regulate the forms of bonsai single or in groups. Before choosing one, however, it is good to look at the plant we have available, looking at it from the height of the pot and not from above, and trying to identify which style best suits its structure.

We are now going to consider all the bonsai styles that are suitable for a single plant. We will describe; Chokkan, Moyogi, Shakan, Kengai, Han-Kengai, and that of the twisted trunk.

Chokkan or erect style- The Chokkan style has a completely straight tree, with the strongest and thickest branches growing to a third of its height and thinning more and more going upwards.

The branches are arranged symmetrically with respect to the trunk and gradually shorten, giving the tree the image of a cone.

Since the branches must always grow parallel to the ground, it is good to apply the metal wire, if necessary. Conifers are the plants that respond most to this style.

Moyogi or curved trunk style-It is a rather simple style to take care of as it is very natural for the tree. The bonsai has a very balanced shape as the trunk grows straight upwards with some slight curvatures.

The branches grow randomly outside the curvatures and gradually thinner to the top.

The most suitable plants for this style are oaks, beeches and maples.

Pruning will tend to give this shape to the tree, especially eliminating the larger branches that grow towards the top of the plant.

Let's now consider those styles that are suitable for groups of bonsai, both those grown from the same root, and those grouped together.

According to Japanese bonsai rules, there should never be a pan number of plants, except for number two.

Sokan or style of the twin trunks- This style concerns two trees grown from the same root.

The tree that has a more robust trunk is usually called the father, the other son.

The point where the two trees join the root must be as low as possible, so as to give the impression that the bonsai is a composition of two completely autonomous plants.

Sankan or triple trunk style - This style is a variant of the previous one since three twin trees branch off from the root, which must have different sizes to recognize a father, the largest, the son, the minor, and the mother, the one intermediate.

Again, the conjunction with the root should be as low as possible.

Kabudachi or multiple trunk styles - Always starting as a base from the Sokan, in this style trees are left to grow from the roots in any odd number greater than three, so as to form a small forest.

It is also necessary to remember for this style the importance of the conjunction of plants with roots.

Ikadabuchi or raft style - According to this style, the tree looks like it has fallen to one side and has begun to root downwards and branch upwards, creating new stems that arise from the ground.

For this style, it is better to choose a plant with many branches on one side of the trunk, by cutting or directing the other branches in the right way.

The main trunk must be arranged horizontally and partially covered with earth, making all the branches come out vertically.

As the months go by, new roots will grow in the lower part of the trunk and it will become necessary to cut the original roots of the tree which, until then, were arranged horizontally.

Netsuranari or sinuous raft style - It is a style that derives from the previous one, from which it differs only for a small feature.

In fact, the trunk of the tree, always arranged horizontally, twists on itself, giving the whole bonsai a sinuous effect.

Yose-ue or forest style -The Yose-ue style refers to the composition of several trees of the same species, but of different ages and sizes, so as to form a miniature forest.

This style requires special preparation and care as, for a good aesthetic result, both spaces and the arrangement of plants must be carefully dosed.

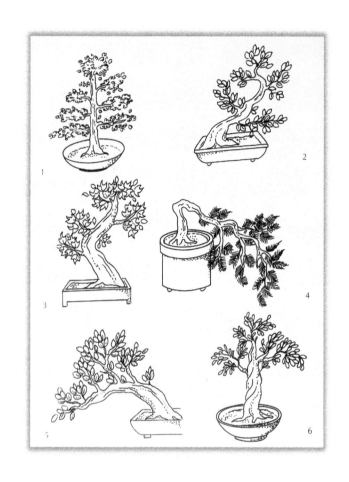

1)Chokkan; 2)Moyogi; 3)Shakan; 4)Kengai;
5)Han-Kengai; 6) Twisted trunk style

44

However, it is possible to define some rules that facilitate the composition.

- First of all, it is good to keep in mind already from which angle you want the bonsai to be observed.

  It is therefore recommended to prepare an approximate drawing of the desired arrangement, so as to study the way to prevent two plants from being covered by each other.

- Usually, the trees are arranged in decreasing order of height: In the foreground the larger ones, the medium ones in the center, and at the bottom the smaller ones.

  This is to give the overall composition a greater three-dimensional effect.

- Always keep in mind that even the empty spaces between the trees have great importance for the harmony of the image.

Great importance also assumes the preparation of the pot in which the bonsai will be planted. This must have a narrow edge and be elongated in shape, large enough to allow each tree adequate root space.

On the bottom of the container, it is necessary to place a wire mesh with tight links, carefully covered with the first layer of gravel and a subsequent layer of bonsai soil.

After arranging the trees, add more soil to the empty spaces and press it carefully.

Both single and group bonsai styles

We will now see the styles that are suitable for both single and group bonsai.

Hokidachi or inverted broom style- The Hokidachi gives the bonsai an appearance reminiscent of an inverted broom, with the branches starting just above the middle of the stem and fan-shaped upwards until reaching the top. The trunk is erect.

The roots must also be thick and robust and distributed harmoniously in the soil.

A tree suitable for this style, however, is not easy to find in nature, therefore the use of metal wire or even the entire development process from cuttings or by layering is recommended so that the desired shape can be reached more precisely.

Fukinagashi or windswept style - It is a style that requires a lot of care to get good results.

It is rather similar to the Shakan, with the trunk inclined diagonally, with the difference that its branches are not arranged on both sides of the trunk, but extend only on the inclination side, so as to give the impression that the tree is prey to the continuous force of the wind.

It is therefore necessary to cut all the branches that grow on the opposite side to the inclination and let the others thicken and grow stronger.

The branches must always develop horizontally. Even the roots, to respect the image of the tree that fights against the wind, must be very robust and well planted in the ground.

Bunjingi or littered style - This style gives greater importance to the trend of the trunk than to the crown. The bonsai, in fact, is completely bare of branches along the entire length of the stem, except on the top, where small branches develop.

The trunk can be totally erect or have more or less pronounced inclinations, but always so as to maintain a certain harmony of form.

1) Sokan, 2) Sankan, 3) Kabudachi, 4) Ikadabuchi,
5) Netsuranari, 6) Yose-ve

Ishitsuki is one of the most fascinating styles of bonsai art, as it requires a certain capacity, in addition to offering a remarkable aesthetic effect.

It is called a rock style because inside the container a rock of variable size is placed, which can have two main functions: Either to be simple support for the roots (Ishitsuki on rock) or to be the place where the roots are rooted (Ishitsuki in the rock).

It is good to use rocks that have strong angles and bright colors in order to give a vital image to the composition.

In the event that a rock does not fully satisfy us from the point of view of the shape, it is possible to work with a chisel to bring it closer to our desires.

As for the containers, the oval ones are shallow, with colors and dimensions in harmony with the structure of the rock and the bonsai.

However, the containers usually have neutral colors to counterbalance the more vivid ones of the rock.

Before starting the real work, it is good, also in this case, to make some preliminary sketches to get an idea of how the final composition will look, studying both the point of view from which the bonsai will be observed, both the natural situation and possibly you want to recreate.

It will also be useful to guarantee the bonsai a long and robust root system so that it easily adapts to the new environment in which it will live.

An easy method is to plant the tree in a very deep container and root it well.

Every 3 months 1inch of soil will be removed from the surface of the pot, while keeping the plant at the original height, in order to leave the roots in the open air and to force them to stretch to look for the nourishment in the soil below, The operation will be repeated until the roots have reached a satisfactory length and the plant will then be ready to become a good rocky bonsai.

Now we will examine the differences between the two cases and show how to make a good rocky bonsai.

Ishitsuki on rock – According to this style, the tree is placed on the top of a medium-small rock with the roots that run along with it until it is planted in the ground, giving the impression of wanting to imprison it.

It is, therefore, necessary to choose a tree that has robust roots and arranged in a sunburst pattern and, once placed on the rock, it will contribute to the harmony of the image by cutting the roots too large or too thin.

The tips of the roots are buried in the ground and the others are stopped at the rock to ensure greater stability for the plant.

To do this, it is recommended to use either tape or a metal wire which will be blocked as much as possible inside the cavities of the rock.

After the arrangement, these roots are covered first with a mixture of clay and peat for the thickness of 1 inch, then with the soil wrapped with muslin bandages, it is good to water abundantly and repeatedly, keeping this layer of the soil always moist. In fact, the plant has a great need for nourishment, since the roots are only partially in contact with the earth.

After about 5 months, or in any case, when the roots are sufficiently developed in the pot, muslin and layer of soil on the rock can be eliminated.

From now on the tree is ready to become a good bonsai.

Ishitsuki in the rock- As for Ishitsuki in the rock, the tree is arranged so that the roots penetrate small cavities and root them.

The rock will, therefore, have dimensions large enough to allow this operation.

The most suitable cavity to hold the bonsai is established and it is filled with a light layer of potting soil which will form the basis for the roots.

The bonsai is placed in the cavity, after cleaning the roots and having them covered with soil and peat.

Anchor the tree with wire, as described in Ishitsuki on the rock, making sure that the wire keeps the roots well adhered to the soil of the cables and that the tree is as firm as possible. If necessary, it is good to anchor in several places.

Also, in this case, the soil is constantly kept humid and care will be taken that the bonsai is not exposed too directly to the sun or wind.

These two art forms are related to the nearby bonsai, as they are for creating particular landscapes.

Saikeiin fact is the art of composing a landscape, combining bonsai with small statuettes, houses and buildings of various types.

To compose a similar aspect, you need an idea of a particular and imaginative scenography on which trees and other elements are displayed, giving the impression of observing a portion of nature in miniature.

It is also necessary to carefully take care of the proportions between the various components, as well as the colors and the perspective.

To dare a more natural and wild aspect it is better than the trees are of different ages and sizes, as for every group bonsai.

Bonkei is used in rock saikei. This composition is of particular importance for the Zen tradition, in fact, it implies an attempt to grasp the deep essence of the rock.

All the difficulty, therefore, lies in enhancing the reading of the composition through the arrangement of the elements, the colors, the shapes, up to obtaining a landscape that knows how to show calm and tranquility but also robustness and vital energy

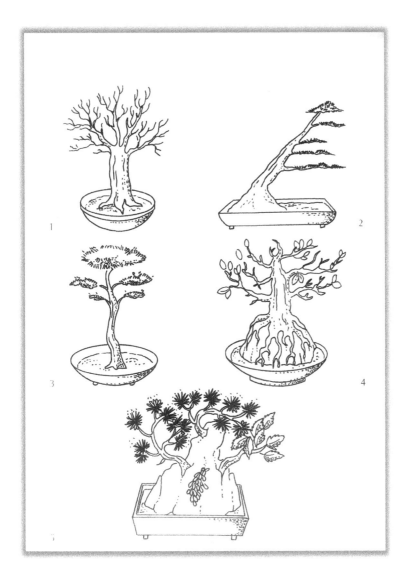

1)Hokidachi; 2) Fukinagashi; 3) Bunjingi; 4)Ishitsuki on the rock; 5) Ishitsuki in the rock

CHAPTER 3 - BONSAI CARE

We are now going to take a closer look at the actual work that characterizes bonsai art, starting from the fundamental part that concerns pruning up to the simplest, but no less important, operations of watering and fertilization.

First of all, it is good to know that bonsai needs daily care and needs, like all plants, to maintain particular rhythms and habits.

The ability of a bonsai artist also lies in being able to respect the woods of his plant. However, there are some rules that it is good to follow to get a good bonsai, and that concern each of the five parts of which a plant is made, starting from the roots to get to the top.

Let's see them in detail:
- **Roots:** It is important that the roots develop in all directions so as to allow a better grip on the ground and more adequate nourishment.
- **Trunk:** The trunks must have a solid and robust base and progressively thin upwards. The older the trunk appears, worn from years and from natural damage, such as cracks in the bark, lightning strikes, the more the bonsai acquires value.
- **Branches:** The branches must have a fixed arrangement, the larger ones must extend to the sides, while the smaller ones upwards. The

branches that grow on the front, those that start from the same point of the trunk, and those that develop horizontally in a regular way are not very appreciated.

- **Leaves:** The leaves must always be proportionate to the rest of the bonsai. They must remain small and cover the branches creating a thick crown.
- **Top:** The top in the bonsai tradition symbolizes life, it must, therefore, be vital and robust. A broken or ruined top is never considered valuable, except when it gives the tree a desired air of austerity.

PRUNING

Pruning is the main job that allows us to keep a small tree, as it gives us the opportunity to modify and control the natural plant development.

By cutting a branch, in fact, it is prevented from continuing to grow and forces them to develop small sub-branches that will form a 10 crown.

However, it is good to consider that there are different ways of pruning depending on the style and the type of tree you want to grow, as we will see later in the data sheets relating to the main bonsai plants.

Before embarking on the pruning operation, you must have a clear understanding of the shape you want to give the plant so that you know where to start.

We take the appropriate tools, such as simple bonsai and bud shears, and get to work, remembering some basic rules, which are indispensable for obtaining the necessary effects of harmony and balance.

First of all, the branches must not grow in the lower part of the trunk.

Usually, the branches are started to develop at a third of the total length of the trunk, to give the plant greater impetus.

It is important to take into great consideration the point where the plant is observed; in this way, it will be evident, as we have seen, that the branches that grow on the front of the plant are useless, while those on the sides and on the back will be accentuated.

To give a livelier image to the bonsai, while maintaining a harmonious appearance, it is good to avoid the branches that grow at the same height and parallel, and also, during pruning, remember not to prune all the branches to the same size, but to leave different lengths.

If you want to limit the growth of a branch, to keep it small, it is sufficient to trim it, otherwise, it will develop and strengthen.

61

It is advisable to carry out pruning in the period of the year in which the crown is developed, so as to have undergone a clear image of the cuts that are being practiced on the bonsai.

Finally, it is very important, when you want to cut a whole branch, as close as possible to the trunk, by leveling the cut, so as to hide the wound from sight.

For this purpose, the use of concave shears is recommended.

In addition, in the case of particularly deep wounds, it is good to use a suitable disinfectant to be purchased from a nurseryman.

Sometimes to give an older image to the bonsai, a special tool is used, called a jinning forceps. This allows the branches to be cut so as to leave part of the bark of the branch attached to the trunk, giving the impression that the tree has been affected by lightning.

For use of pruning to direct the growth of branches. By pruning the branch, a just above a bud facing downwards we will obtain a branch that will grow upwards after drawing a curve.

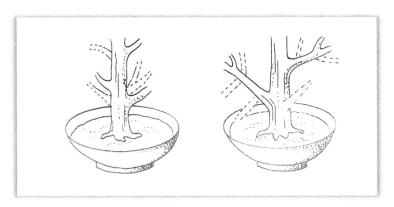

The dashes in the two sequences, show the branches that are of no use for the formation of any bonsai style, therefore they must be pruned.

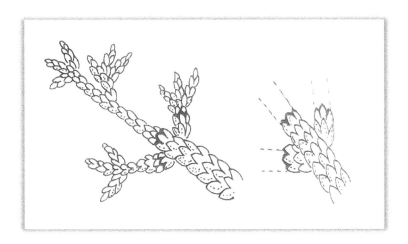

How to trim the shoots of a conifer

Effects of leaf pruning

This technique is particularly difficult and still requires some experience in order not to ruin the plant.

Cutting leaves and buds

It happens that an indoor bonsai throws the buds all year round, so pruning leaves and buds are an almost daily practice.

However, it is easy to apply, in fact, the rules to follow are less numerous than for pruning branches. The important thing is to remember that where a sprout is left there, a branch will develop, while the lower part of the trunk will be strengthened and the branching will become thinner.

In any case, it is good to remember that the leaves must always be cut leaving a piece of a stalk and that the direction of the last leaf a stalk left after cutting also determines the direction of the bud that will grow later.

It is recommended to always cut the biggest leaves. As for the plants that bloom, pruning will only be done after the development of the flowers.

While for subtropical plants the right period for cutting shoots and leaves is between spring and autumn, tropical plants, which grow all year round, will always be pruned and pruned.

In conifers, the topping of the shoots, an operation sometimes performed simply with the nails, will cause many small needles to develop. In short, the cutting of the leaves allows us to obtain three main results: A thin branching, the shrinking of the leaves and greater ventilation of the crown of the branches.

Every year, in the period between March and August, it is good to proceed with the total defoliation of the tree; in doing so, the plant is stimulated to develop new shoots in a short time, accelerating vegetative growth.

Smaller leaves and thinner branches will grow under the petioles, giving the bonsai the classic appearance of a dwarf tree.

We now pass to another very important moment, that of the application of the metal wire, which is essential for the tree to grow according to the desired shape.

Suitable wires are copper or aluminum and for some types of trees, such as maple, apricot and thorns, it is convenient to use plastic-coated threads or wrapped in paper.

The diameter will be of different sizes depending on the thickness and strength of the branch to be corrected.

Usually, a wire 1/3 of the diameter of the branch or trunk to be wrapped is used.

Before proceeding with the application, it is advisable to fix the wire to the ground or to the trunk, always starting from the backside, so as to hide the origin of the binding or not to leave too much play.

Especially for the first case, in fact, it would damage the bark of the tree, risking the wire embedding itself in the bonsai. In this case, it is better to cut the metal wire and leave the part embedded in the shaft, to avoid even greater injuries.

The wire should be wound at an angle of 45 degrees Celsius - 113 Fahrenheit, to the trunk or branch, avoiding tying both leaves and buds.

The period of time in which to maintain the binding is different depending on the style chosen

67

and the type of tree: Indicatively, it varies from 6-8 months of deciduous plants to 18 months of conifers.

The thread will preferably be removed in the autumn before the vegetative stasis. It is good to remember not to apply during the vegetative awakening of the plant, not to practice it on newly repotted or repotted bonsai trees, as each of these operations considerably weakens the plant.

Once the wire has been applied, the plant will be kept in a place sheltered from the sun and wind, spraying and watering often.

The metal wire is the main technique for changing the shape of the plant; however, there are other ways to correct it.

In fact, you can also use cords attached to the container, to another support, or to the trunk itself to keep the branches in tension.

Other times stones or weights can be tied to a branch in order to change its direction of development.

Finally, with small wooden dowels, it is possible to spread two branches considered too close.

Of all these techniques, however, that of the metal wire is the most used, as it allows a more precise action on the branches and on the trunk.

Transplanting and repotting

We will now deal with that part of the bonsai care that concerns transplanting, that is moving the plant from one soil to another, and repotting, that is, moving from one container to another,

Transplanting has the utility of providing new fertile soil and chemical balanced to the plant.

The earth is gradually depleted by the tree that uses mineral substances as nourishment. It is therefore necessary to replace it with new soil to prevent the plant from weakening or wasting.

The main purpose of the repotting instead is to limit the size of the roots, favoring the development of rootlets which, although small in size, provide most of the nourishment to the plant.

For each repotting, therefore, you can use a smaller pot, or at the maximum keep the size of the previous pot. However, it is good to prepare the container, sterilizing it from germs, and cover it.

I give the drainage holes with a thin mesh metal mesh, so as to allow the water to pass without the soil coming out.

If the container is very high, a drainage layer of about 1inch must be created using pebbles.

This will allow the water not to stagnate. It should be remembered that the right period for repotting is the beginning of spring, except for tropical and subtropical plants which can be repotted at any time of the year.

Besides, young plants must be repotted every year, to accompany their rapid growth, while the older ones can wait even two or three years. It is however good to note that the plant needs repotting when the soil rises above the edge of the container due to the thrust that the roots provide. Repotting should be started when the soil is dry, so you can work more easily. Here's how it goes.
You turn the pot upside down and, holding the bonsai by the trunk, hit the bottom of the container so as to gently let the soil out with the roots.

After bringing the bonsai back in the right direction, proceed to clean the roots of the residual earth and shorten those too long by a third. The main root, the larger one, will be checked and dead or too weak roots will be eliminated.

After pruning, the container is filled with a thin layer of soil and the bonsai is placed in the pot, taking the measures for a correct arrangement: The root of the roots must not exceed the edge of the pot.

Pour more soil into the container without exceeding, pressing it to make it adhere well to the root system, and proceed with watering, taking care not to create grooves in the ground, and placing the pot in a sheltered place.

However, it is recommended not to use the fertilizer for at least one or two months after repotting.

It is good now to spend a few words about the ideal soil for bonsai, so as to provide each plant with the best nutritional intake and the best possibility of development.

The most suitable soil is absolutely the original one of the plants, although none is always easy to dispose of.

Therefore, different types of soil must be purchased to have a suitable mixture.

how to wrap the wire around the trunk and branches

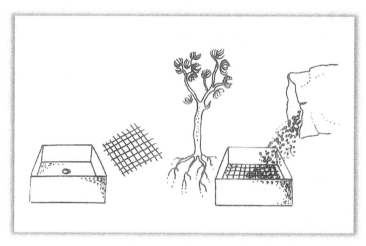

Application of metal mesh for drainage

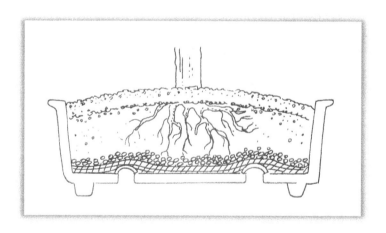

Drainage in a tall container with wire mesh and pebbles

In case you already have available the earth and you run the risk that contains insect eggs, you will have to spread it in the sun so that the eggs die.

You can also sterilize the earth with fingers or chloropicrin.

Bonsai soil is a mixture of various elements, such as peat, sand and clay. Each of these elements gives the soil certain characteristics, the clay is the actual greasy soil, and the peat provides the humus while the sand allows the soil to breathe more easily and chooses water.

However, each plant has certain needs, due to the speed of growth, the need for humidity, and above all the degree of acidity of the soil.

Acidity is a very important element for the good development of the plant, therefore, it must be carefully observed. We recommend the purchase of a pH-meter, of the mixture, so as to offer the best soil to the plant.

A large quantity of plants prefers an acidity degree between 5.5 and 6 on the pH meter scale.

We can schematize the degree of acidity necessary for the various plants in this way: Device for measuring acidity;

- PH less than 3.7: Plants that grow in areas with acidic soil.
- PH between 3.8 and 4.5: Spruce, Canadian fir, birch and poplar.
- PH between 4.6 and 5.5: Most conifers.
- PH between 5.6 and 6.9: Almost all deciduous trees.

- PH between 7.0 and 8.0: Plants that live in neutral or alkaline grasslands.

If there are imbalances between the plant and the soil, the mixture must be modified, adding a lot of peat, a very acidic substance, if we want to increase the acidity degree, or removing it, if we want to decrease it, possibly adding lime or calcium carbonate, so as to correct it further.

However, general rules can be laid down on the composition of the mixture for some plants. For example, young plants, or in general deciduous that have rather rapid growth, need more oily soil, therefore a mixture consisting of 1/3 of clay, 1/3 of peat, and 1/3 0 sand is recommended. Slow-growing plants, like conifers, need more sandy soil, so the mixture should be 1/4 clay, 1/4 peat 2/4 sand. However, it is good to sift the final mixture in order to and the soil agglomerates, making it uniform and homogeneous.

After filling the container, it is good practice to also apply the last layer of pulverized moss or leaf soil mixed with soil to give a more natural and wilder image to the creation

Watering is another very important phase in the care of a bonsai. It must be practiced often with extreme care, so as not to damage the plant. The bonsai, in fact, because of its restricted root system, it does not draw sustenance from the soil for a long time.

It is therefore necessary to keep it supplied with moist soil rich in nutrients. It is a good rule to water the soil only when it is dry or slightly damp; watering when the soil is still wet can cause more damage than advantages.

Some tricks allow us, however, to easily understand if it is really necessary to water. The first concerns the color that the soil takes on: it will be drier the more the color becomes clear.

A dark color instead indicates that the earth is still steeped in water.

The need for water from the bonsai can also be ascertained by simply knocking against the container and listening to the sound produced.

Usually, an empty sound shows that the earth has dried up, detaching itself from the edges of the vase; on the contrary, a full muffled sound will indicate that the earth is dilated by water and adheres well to the container.

Two methods are mainly used for watering: Either the water is poured onto the soil surface through a watering can, or the container is directly immersed in the water. In the first case, it will be necessary to proceed slowly, to allow time for the soil to fully impregnate.

When the water comes out of the drain hole, the soil will have been properly watered. In the event, however, that the water cannot penetrate the soil, but escapes from the edge of the container, it means that the earth is too dry and we will proceed in the other way.

The second method is equally simple. The containers are immersed in water to bring bubbles of air to the surface. When no more bubbles come out, the soil will be completely drenched with water and the bonsai can be rearranged in its place.

The bonsai however change their water needs in the changing seasons. In summer it will be necessary to water more frequently, at least twice a day, making sure that the soil does not dry out too much. However, we recommend watering early in the morning and in the evening with water at room temperature.

Furthermore, especially in the city, it is important to spray the leaves during the day to eliminate the smog and dust layer that can be created. However, you have to remember not to do it in the evening, because the plant could get sick or be damaged in any case.

Furthermore, during the summer period, miniature and rock bonsai trees need more water than normal bonsai, as well as deciduous trees since the rather large surface of the leaves increases transudation.

In the autumn season, however, the need for water decreases, the leaves fall, and the plant prepares for winter stasis. In any case, it will be good to frequently check the humidity conditions in order not to experience unpleasant inconveniences.

With winter, the phase of least demand for water is reached, as the tree slows down most of its functions and enters a period of substantial inactivity.

It is therefore sufficient to water 2-3 times a week, preferably during the afternoon hours to avoid night frost.

Only conifers maintain their need for water rather high since the foliar apparatus does not fall during the autumn and needs continuous nourishment.

With spring, however, the full activity of the tree begins again, the shoots reappear and the demand for water resumes, which will increase more and more over time, as we get closer to summer.

Fertilizers, if used correctly, are indispensable to help the development of our bonsai, by integrating and completing the nutrients of the soil.

Deprived of fertilizers the bonsai would live for about a year, therefore it would begin to perish, the leaves would wither and branches and trunk would weaken.

This is because the bonsai, being forced into a pot of such a small size after a certain period exhausts the mineral elements necessary for its nourishment.

It is therefore important to remember that every bonsai needs a certain amount of nitrogen, phosphorus, potassium, calcium, sulfur, iron and, in smaller quantities, other minerals.

We will, therefore, have to look for fertilizers that contain these substances.

Various types of fertilizers are available on the market: Powder, liquids and balls, the latter used mainly for outdoor bonsai but also very suitable for indoor bonsai.

Furthermore, a distinction is also made between organic fertilizers, namely those derived from organic fabrics, such as bone meal, blood-based fertilizers, etc., and inorganic fertilizers, such as salt compounds.

For good fertilization, it is however essential to follow some rules.

First of all, the fertilizer should be administered especially during the growing season of the plant, helping it with all the necessary nourishment; it is, the youngest bonsai to need more help, precisely for their very rapid growth.

During the growth period, fertilization must be carried out every twenty days, going as far as fertilizing also every week, during the autumn, to prepare the plant for the winter period. In winter, fertilization is superfluous for many bonsai as the plant stops its vegetative development.

Only conifers are to be fertilized as early as January as they resume activity before other plants. Fertilization should always be carried out after the flowering period, to prevent the flowering branches from absorbing too much nourishment and losing the flowers. Remember also that it is good not to start immediately after repotting or pruning the roots, as the injured parts would be damaged.

Once you have chosen the most suitable period and the type of fertilizer you can move on to the practical phase.

Water abundantly and prepare the dose of fertilizer as indicated on the package; in fact, the dose for a bonsai does not differ much from that normally recommended.

This is how we proceed to fertilization, remembering these tips:

- It is always better to fertilize little, but often, rather than a lot and rarely because in this way the food is distributed more regularly over time, without risking excesses.
- Liquid fertilizers are absorbed faster, so it will be necessary to fertilize more often. On the contrary, powder fertilizers dissolve more slowly in the soil, allowing a lasting effect.

If the roots get sick, it is good to stop fertilizing until the root system is completely restored

CHAPTER 4 - PLANT DISEASES

We now begin a very important chapter in the care of bonsai, as it can often happen that a plant shows symptoms of a disease that is difficult to recognize and, therefore, to cure. In fact, due to its size, the bonsai is more defenseless than the normal plants against the attacks of many adversities, therefore it is the bonsai artist's job to quickly recognize the diseases and help his plant.

When the bonsai begins to weaken, it is immediately necessary to check whether there are deficiencies or excesses of some kind in its care and maintenance: In what position is the plant about to the wind and light? At what level are humidity and temperature? Is it fed in the right way? All these factors must always be kept under control, but sometimes the bad health of our bonsai can derive from other causes.

It is important to bear in mind that bonsai are subject to the same pests and diseases as the species of the trees to which they belong. Therefore, in principle, as regards diseases due to plant or animal parasites, a bonsai, if in full force, has the potential to defend itself.

A constant cure would, therefore, be sufficient to prevent and avoid diseases of this type.

However, this does not exclude that, during the weakening phases due to repotting or pruning, the bonsai can get sick.

Among the animal parasites, we find various types of insects that damage the plant by using it for their nourishment.

The most common are:

- **Laniger aphid and white cochineal**
  Description: They are small insects that develop at the expense of the plant, surrounding themselves with a white waxy substance and feeding on the sap.
  Symptoms: White and woolly formations wrap around the petioles of the leaves and the divergence of the branches, weakening the plant.
  Cure: Use Croneton or Compron on the soil, or water with Ekamet or Proposcur at 0.15%.
- **Black aphid**

Description: It is an insect that lives in colonies, spreading especially in spring and creating blackish formations attached to sheets and flowers. This slows down the development of the plant in the affected areas.

Symptoms: Dark windings hit the shoots and stretch to the leaves and flowers.

Cure: Use Croneton and Primor without affecting the flowers.

- **Cochineal**

Description: It is an insect that feeds on the sap of plants, injecting a chemical substance inside that causes an abundant secretion of sugars.

Symptoms: In the lower part of the leaves dark-colored folds are created.

Care: It would sometimes be sufficient to remove the animals from the plant with a simple stick, however, the use of Primor or 0.2% Aphisan, sprayed on the plant, or Croneton poured into the ground is recommended.

- **Phylloxeraradicicol**

Description: It is a female aphid of small size, green or yellow-brown, which lays a large number of eggs and attacks the roots of plants.

Symptoms: The plant tends to turn yellow and deteriorate. Looking at the roots or the earth, one can notice small gray-white ball formations.

Cure: Pour on the ground of Croneton or a solution of Metasystox or Alphos.

- **Whitefly or Aleuroids**

  Description: The whitefly is a white insect whose larvae, hidden under the leaves, feed on the sap of the plant, forcing it to emit various sugary productions. It mainly affects plants such as Lantana and Segerezia.

  Symptoms: The leaves begin to turn yellow at the bottom and weaken.

  Care: The use of products such as Folithion, Ambush, or Undene is recommended.

- **Lice or aphids**

  Description: Lice and aphids are insects that live in rather large groups, attaching themselves to the trunk and leaves to suck the sap. Some species are equipped with wings and, moving from plant to plant, they also favor the spread of viruses. **Symptoms:** Insect groups cover leaves and buds that weaken and decay.

  Cure: There may be enough water to remove them. Otherwise use Primor or Croneton, or spray with Parexan or another spray.

- **Red spider or garden mite**

  Description: They are small red, yellow or brown spiders that make their nests on the leaves on the branches. They attack both fruit trees and plants of other species.

  Symptoms: The leaves are wrapped in very thin cobwebs on which it is possible to notice animals with a lens. Over time the leaves turn yellow and weaken.

Cure: We recommend using Tetagril on the ground, or spraying the plant with special Lizetan or Metasystox R, particularly suitable against these insects.

Plant parasites are caused by conditions of the particular weakness of the plant that facilitate the spread of diseases.

The main ones are:

- *Chlorosis*

Description: It is a disease due to a lack of iron or excess calcium in the soil. Factors that prevent easy absorption of mineral substances cause a serious deficiency of chlorophyll inside the plant.

Symptoms: The leaves begin to turn yellow, but leave the ribs green, and wither.

Cure: Before watering, pour Fetrilon or Sequestrene into the right amount.

- *Sooty mold*

Description: They are fungi that affect the bonsai in the trunk, in the leaves and the branches, giving rise to dark incrustations. Mushrooms often feed on sugary substances caused by the passage of aphids and above all are favored by high humidity and poor ventilation.

Symptoms: Dark-colored spots or sooty areas are created in the affected areas.

Cure: We recommend the use of Cupravit or Baymat, or in any case of any product with copper oxychloride.

- **Radical rot**

Description: The roots rot mainly for two reasons: Excessive fertilization, which causes damage and necrosis, and an excessively abundant watering, which causes water to stagnate in the soil.

Symptoms: The plant weakens and begins to perish, due to the Tadice's inability to forfeit nourishment, the leaves take on a dark color.

Cure: It is good to cut the sick and already dead roots and leave the healthy ones in a solution of Benomyl or Orthocid, after having cleaned them well from the ground.

Kiplantate the bonsai in a pot with new soil, keeping the soil watered and moist fertilizing should be practiced only after 2 months.

- **Powdery mildew or Spaerotheca**

Description: They are also fungi that affect the plant in particular conditions of temperature and ventilation. Their propagation is facilitated by the particular heat and humidity, so it is good to be particularly careful in the summer.

Symptoms: Powdery mildew creates a whitish powder-like substance on the front of the leaves and in the other affected points, gradually weakening the plant.

Cure: To eliminate powdery mildew in a short time, you can use any fungicide or even a KB solution of micronized sulfur to be administered every 15 days.

- **_False powdery mildew_**

Description: It is a mushroom similar to the previous one, even if it manifests itself differently way. It is favored by inadequate conditions of temperature and humidity.

Symptoms: It determines a gray moldy substance in the lower part of the leaves, while it turns yellow the upper one, staining some points of gray.

Cure: Use Bayleton or CupravitBlu, spraying it in the relevant points, transporting the bonsai to a well-ventilated place

- **_Virosis_**

Description: These are all the diseases caused by the spread of viruses which, however, are still not easily identifiable today and which often occur in a deleterious way for plants.

The virus spreads easily or through insects, or due to infected tools, or in any circumstance in which some wounds of the tree can be affected, such as in the case of grafts, pruning, etc.

Symptoms: The symptoms are various and are not always recognizable in a short time. In the most common cases, these are streaks of various colors that are highlighted on the leaves; regardless of the symptoms the fate of the plant is however probably sealed.

Cure: Unfortunately, there are few remedies after a plant has been affected.

You can only try to make sure that the infection does not expand, moving the plant away. Above all, however, it is recommended to prevent virosis by fighting animal parasites and keeping tools clean.

Bonsai must always be placed in an environment suitable for its needs. Each species requires a certain amount of light, humidity, temperature, which must be guaranteed overtime for the good health of the plant. Let's see together how to give our bonsai the optimal environment.

Temperature

It is good to always keep in mind the temperature of the original place of the plant and try to recreate it also in our apartment.

Plants are classified into two groups, depending on their origin and needs: Tropical plants and subtropical plants.

Tropical plants need during the day temperature between 18 and 24 degrees Celsius - 64.4-75,2 Fahrenheit; at night it is better not to drop below 15-16 degrees Celsius – 60 Fahrenheit.

The subtropical plants, on the other hand, do not bear a too hot climate, and I prefer minimum temperatures in winter between 5 and 12 degrees Celsius - 41-53,6 Fahrenheit.

Not respecting these needs of the plant means causing them serious damage.

In general, the cold causes a slowdown in growth, chlorosis, cracking of the branches or the trunk, the death of the leaves, even the death of all the bonsai.

It also happens if the temperature is too hot with the risk the plant ends up drying out.

We, therefore, recommend keeping bonsai in a suitable place: Tropical plants are usually placed on heating sources or as close as possible, to exploit their heat throughout the day.

At night it is good to take them to a slightly cooler place, to cause a natural temperature, drop of 5-6 degrees Celsius – 41-42.8 Fahrenheit.

Subtropical plants are more suitable for winter gardens, cool rooms, or in the corridor.

Also, in this case, it is recommended to provide a slight drop in temperature during the night by bringing the plant near the window or in a cooler place.

It is good, however, that the temperature changes are not excessive.

If you intend to place the plants in the open air for the summer, it will be better not to expose them directly to sunlight, they will necessarily be collected at home when the night temperature starts to drop below l degrees.

Light

Plants, as we know, have a great need for light to be able to start the process of photosynthesis, but in this case, too it is good not to exceed.

The excess of light in especially if the plant is not used to it can cause the discoloration of the leaves and a consequent weakening of the plant.

We, therefore, recommend keeping the bonsai in a bright place, without it being directly exposed to the sun's rays.

In the home it is often necessary to use artificial light to integrate the one coming from outside; in this case, it is better to avoid normal incandescent bulbs because they emit light too different from the solar one.
We rather recommend quartz and iodine lamps and fluorescent tubes for aquariums.

Humidity

Two factors can come into play by damaging the plant, if not kept under constant control: The humidity of the air and the watering.

Most bonsai need a humidity of between 40 and 50%.

If the bonsai is placed in a too dry place, the plant evaporates more water than it manages to forfeit from the roots, causing a decrease in growth and risking the leaves, branches and trunk to dry out.

On the contrary, on the other hand, if the humidity is excessive, there is a danger of a general weakening of the plant, of the spread of parasitic diseases such as fungi, up to the possibility that the whole plant will rot. As we said, watering also plays an important role and should be practiced in moderation.

Excess water with bad drainage in the soil facilitates root rot, fungi and pests. It also decreases the speed of development of the plant, causing it asphyxiation and heaviness.

It is therefore better to water often, but in moderate quantities, rather than rarely in large quantities. It is also good to make sure that the water does not stagnate in the pot, but has an easy outlet thanks to the drainage holes.

DISEASES DUE TO EXCESS OR LACK OF NUTRIENTS

Plants can also get sick when the soil does not adequately contain all the elements necessary for nourishment. The bonsai highlights particular symptoms that can become real diseases if you don't try to live the problem immediately with adequate fertilizer. Often, then, the lack of water causes serious damage to leaves and flowers, such as the drying out of the log edges, deformation and fall of the shoots, etc. On the contrary, too much water prevents the soil from breathing, causing root rot.

Now we will examine the nutrients that can cause damage to the plant if they are not present in the necessary quantity.

- **Nitrogen**

  If the soil contains an excessive amount of nitrogen, the tree tends to accelerate its development speed, but this causes a weakening of the plant and a lower ability to defend against disease and cold. If instead the percentage of nitrogen is lower, the development slows down and the vegetative cycle is shortened, to the detriment of leaves and shoots.

- **Boron**

  The lack of boron damages the leaves which weaken, drying out easily.

The plant deteriorates and does not grow.

- **Iron**

  Iron in small quantities causes the leaves to turn yellow and weaken the plant.

- **Phosphorus**

  The lack of phosphorus in the soil causes the plant to stop developing, giving the leaves a bronze color and making them leathery.

- **Magnesium**

  The lack of magnesium in the soil gives the leaves red and chlorosis coloring.

- **Potassium**

  When the plant lacks the right amount of potassium, serious damage to the leaves occurs. They begin to curl on the edges and turn dark and rot; the whole plant suffers, weakening its defenses.

- **Zinc**

  The plant slows down its development, with the consequence that the leaves remain small and thin and easily affected by chlorosis.

Let's talk now about how-to bring relief to the plant in case of injuries caused by diseases or by bad use of tools.

It is first of all important to try to prevent the possibility of injury by keeping the bonsai in a sheltered place, where there is no risk of damage. Also, it is always good to keep the tools in good condition and, during pruning, make a clean and flat cut, to limit the extent of the wound to a minimum.

Plants have a great natural healing ability, however, always good to help them by applying waxes and pastes that contain healing hormones such as Lac balsam or other products readily available on the market.

In case there are dead or infected parts, it is good to remove them immediately, in order to facilitate the recovery of the plant.

Furthermore, during the vegetative period and especially when it is very hot, the plant must be followed in a particular way because it is more active and more willing to infections.

CHAPTER 5 - CONTAINERS AND TOOLS

The choice of the container can compromise or enhance the overall harmony of bonsai creation. An ideal container can bring out a plant without particular value, hiding its defects and highlighting its most peculiar characteristics.

Usually, they are made in porcelain or terracotta and it is not uncommon to find vitrified models on the outside.

However, the containers on the market offer such a variety, of colors and sizes, that the choice is not always easy. However, some rules can help us.

The suitable dimensions depend on those of the bonsai: The pot must be at least two-thirds of the height of the trunk and the height should not be less than the thickness of the trunk.

As for the color, we usually tend to create particular contrasts between the container and the tree, as required by the principle of asymmetric balancing. So, for trees with dark foliage, vases with light colors will be used mostly and vice versa.

This rule is however subject to the taste of the bonsai artist, who may deem preferable, which among other things, in some cases is necessary for a good overall object. Each style prefers a certain shape of the container:

- **Moyogi:** Oval, shallow, round, shallow and rectangular containers can be used.

- **Chokkan:** Shallow, oval and rectangular square pots are to be used.
- **Shakan:** Shallow, round, shallow and rectangular shapes are recommended.
- **Kengai:** Containers must be very deep rounds to allow the tree to develop properly alongside the pot.
- **Sokan:** The containers can be oval and round low
- **Sankan:** The recommended containers are the low shapeless ones.
- **Vahudachi:** Low round, rectangular and low shapeless vases are used.
- **Ikada:** Oval and low-form ones are suitable.
- **Netsuranari:** Shapeless low vessels are recommended.
- **Vose-ue:** The containers must be oval, rectangular or low-form.
- **Hokidachi:** Oval, shallow square, low round and shallow, rectangular and low shapeless containers are to be used.
- **Fukinagashi:** The recommended shapes are oval, shallow square, low round and shallow and rectangular.
- **Bunjingi:** Low and shallow round pots are recommended.
- **Ishitsuki**: The oval, low round and rectangular vases fit.

- **Saikei and Bonkei:** It is preferable to use low oval and rectangular vases, even if all those containers that enhance the general composition are suitable.
- **Han-Kengai:** Use deep or very deep square or very deep round vases.

The use of containers with feet is preferable, because keeping the vase raised concerning the support surface, it allows better air circulation and more easy expulsion of water.

Often the bonsai are placed on special wooden display tables or mobile shelves. The latter, which is useful for moving the plant when necessary, can also be easily built on their own.

Arrangement of bonsai in the container

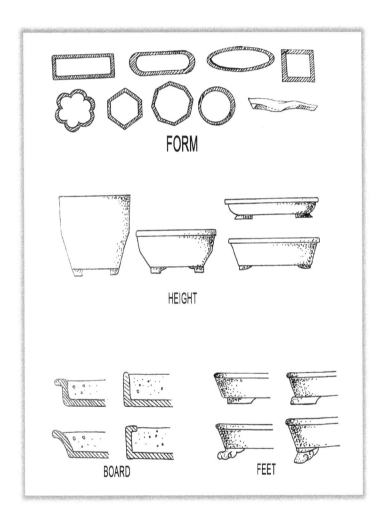

FORM

HEIGHT

BOARD   FEET

After having seen the variety of containers, let's now see together some general advice on which arrangement is best to give the bonsai in their container.

To facilitate the exposure, it is good to make a first distinction between the front and the back of the bonsai. The front is visible to the observer.

It will be necessary, therefore, to choose as the front of the bonsai that part that does not have branches directed towards the observer, to give an orderly and accurate impression to the composition.

Usually, then the roots that emerge from the ground are also placed towards the front, to give an idea of greater stability to the whole plant.

It is also essential to distinguish between straight trunk trees, leaning trunk trees and groups of trees.

Each of these cases will follow different rules:

- **Straight trunk trees:** If your style includes trees with a straight trunk you will have to arrange the trunk so that it is moved a little back from the center of the pot and is slightly inclined towards you. This will result in a lively aspect, accentuating the shape of the crown concerning the tea
- **Tree with leaning trunk:** The inclination of the tree must always be oriented right to left or the other way around. In case the tree leans to the right, you will have to move the base of the trunk to the left of the container. Otherwise, instead, you have to move the trunk to the right of the container. Also, for this group of trees, it

is advisable to bring a slight inclination towards the front

- **_Groups of trees:_** If you have chosen trees that have double or multiple trunks coming from the same root, these will always be arranged in the center of the container. If instead the trees are autonomous from each other and you want to make a composition, they can be arranged in a more varied way.

In this regard, however, more information can be found in the chapter dedicated to group styles.

Bonsai tools

Let's now describe the main tools to be used in the maintenance and transformation of bonsai. For those who are preparing to start growing a bonsai, the following tools are needed:

1. A plastic or metal watering can equip with replaceable onions with a flat and inclined face. The first provides a strong enough jet, useful for watering leaves and foliage. The second is to be used to water the soil as it makes the water flow more gently.
2. A pair of elongated bonsai pruning shears. The length of these elongated allows you to work inside the foliage very easily.
3. A pair of wide scissors, useful for truncating large roots. A bonsai hacksaw can also be used for this purpose.
4. A pair of concave shears, useful for cutting branches to obtain a section as regular as possible, facilitating wound healing.
5. Mesh in thin mesh to be placed over the drainage holes, to prevent lumps of earth from coming out.
6. Aluminum wire to wrap branches and trunk, in case you want to change its shape.
7. A small wire cutter to cut the wire without injuring the bark.

8. A stick or a paperclip to clean the roots from the ground and separate them during repotting.
9. A rake to level the ground.
10. A broom to clean.

It is essential to remember to carefully clean each tool after use to avoid the spread of germs or diseases. For this purpose, it is possible to find types of disinfectants for tools on the market.

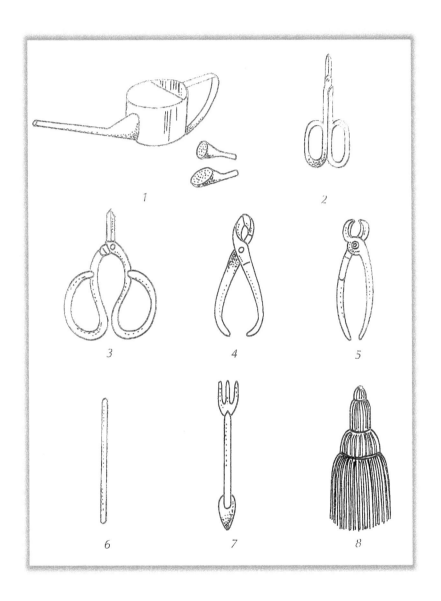

Bonsai tools: 1) Watering can; 2) Elongated scissors; 3) Wide scissors; 4) Concave shears; 5) Nippers; 6) Stick; 7) Rake; 8) Broom

CHAPTER 6 - TIPS AND INFORMATION

When the holiday season arrives, you will face the problem of how to behave with bonsai, where to leave it, whom to leave it, etc. Always comes up.

The ideal would be to have someone to whom to entrust him who is able to replace our care for the necessary period, however, this is not always possible. In the event that the absence is short-lived, lasting up to a week, then the bonsai can be left alone, even if it is necessary to prepare a suitable place to keep it moist all the time. It will be sufficient to bury the pot inside a larger container that has a layer of wet peat. Otherwise, you can create a small greenhouse with a transparent plastic bag inside which to insert the pot. The bag will be closed over the bonsai after it has been watered abundantly. It is also necessary to drill holes in the plastic to circulate the air while maintaining the necessary humidity inside.

For longer periods, a connection can be made between a container full of water, placed higher up, and the bonsai pot using a tube that slowly brings water to a wedge planted in the soil.

To obtain the same result in an easier way, a simple woolen thread can be used instead of the tube and the wedge impregnating the water with the thread, it will slowly let it drop on the ground.

However, even in this case, a person's assistance would be needed to check that everything is going well and to solve any problems that could arise.

1) Watering by subtracting the bonsai pot in a moist soil; 2) Watering through a wire of wool connected to a basin of water; 3) Greenhouse made with perf
orated plastic bag

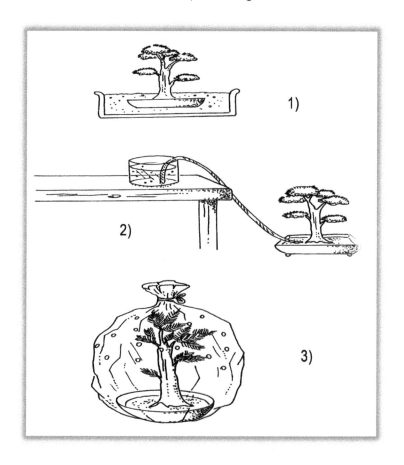